MOONS, MOONS AND MORE MOONS!
ALL MOONS OF OUR SOLAR SYSTEM
SPACE FOR KIDS
CHILDREN'S AERONAUTICS & SPACE BOOK

BABY PROFESSOR

EDUCATION KIDS

Speedy Publishing LLC
40 E. Main St. #1156
Newark, DE 19711
www.speedypublishing.com

Copyright 2015

There are 181
natural moons in our
Solar System.

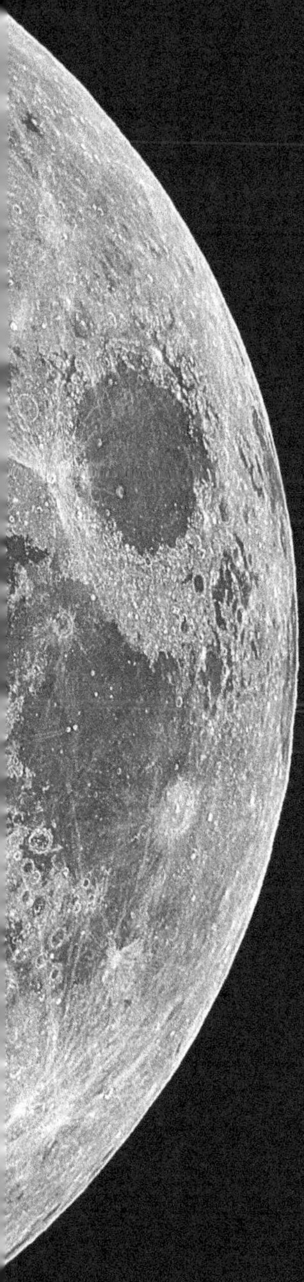

The Moon is the Earth's natural satellite. A satellite is a space body that orbits around a planet.

Deimos is
one of the
two moons
that orbit
Mars. It
is farther
from Mars.

Phobos orbits closer to Mars. Phobos was discovered in 1877 by Asaph Hall.

Ganymede is
one of the
many moons
of Jupiter.
It was
first seen
by Galileo
in 1610.

Callisto is
also one of
Jupiter's
moons.
Callisto may
be one of
the oldest
bodies in
the Solar
System.

Io is the fifth moon from the planet Jupiter. Io has active volcanoes.

Europa is
the sixth
moon from
Jupiter.
Europa is
covered
with thick
layer of ice.

Titan is the largest moon of Saturn. It is also the second largest moon in the solar system.

Mimas
completes
its orbit
around
Saturn in
23 hours.

Rhea is the second largest moon of Saturn. It was discovered by Giovanni Cassini in 1672.

Enceladus is also one of Saturn's moons. It was discovered by William Herschel in 1789.

Iapetus is Saturn's large moon. Iapetus has one side that is bright and the other side is dark.

Titania is the largest moon of Saturn. It is also the eighth largest moon in our solar system.

Oberon
is the
outermost
moon of
Uranus.
Oberon is
made of ice
and rock.

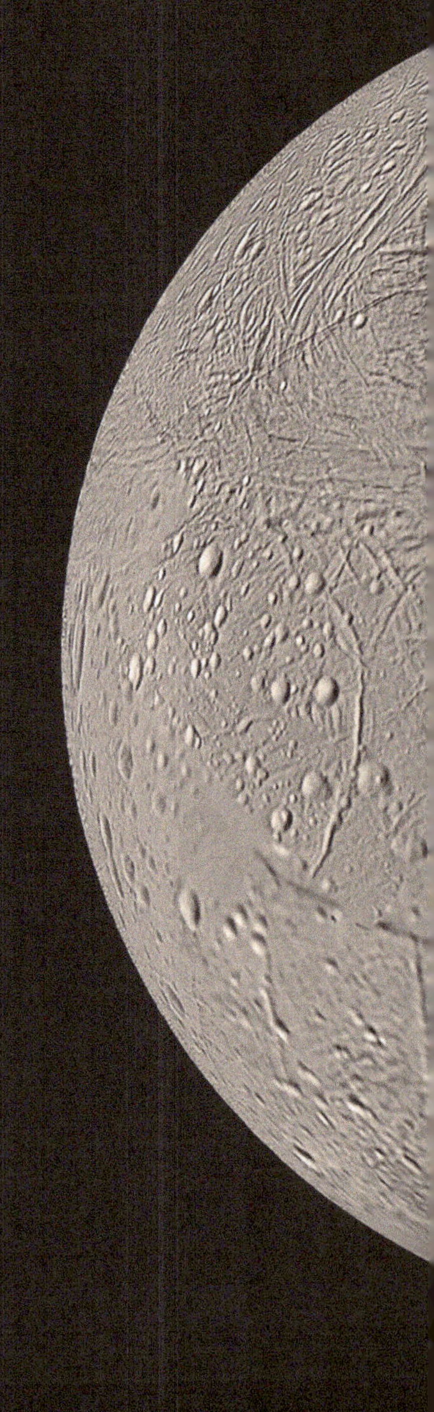

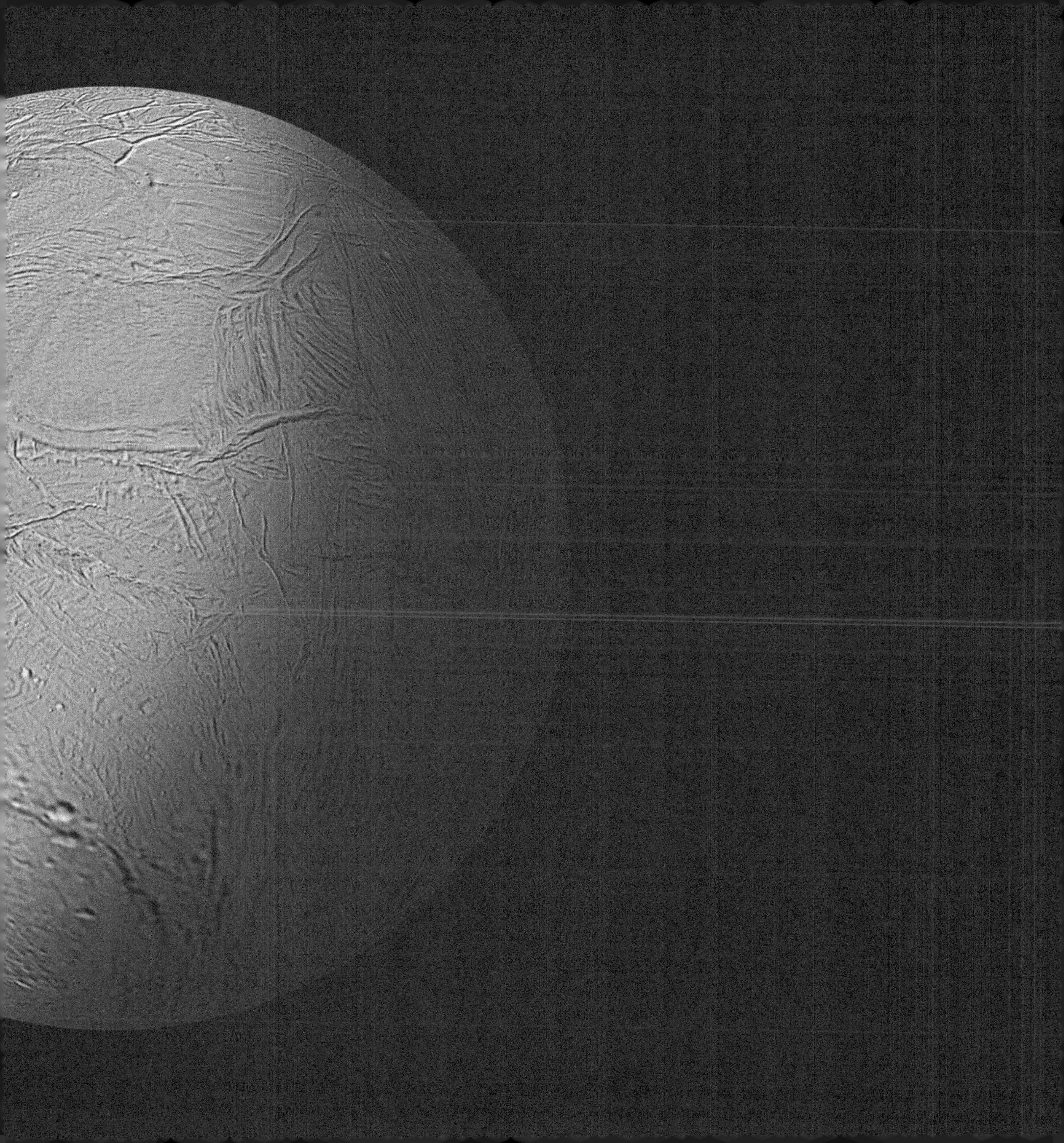

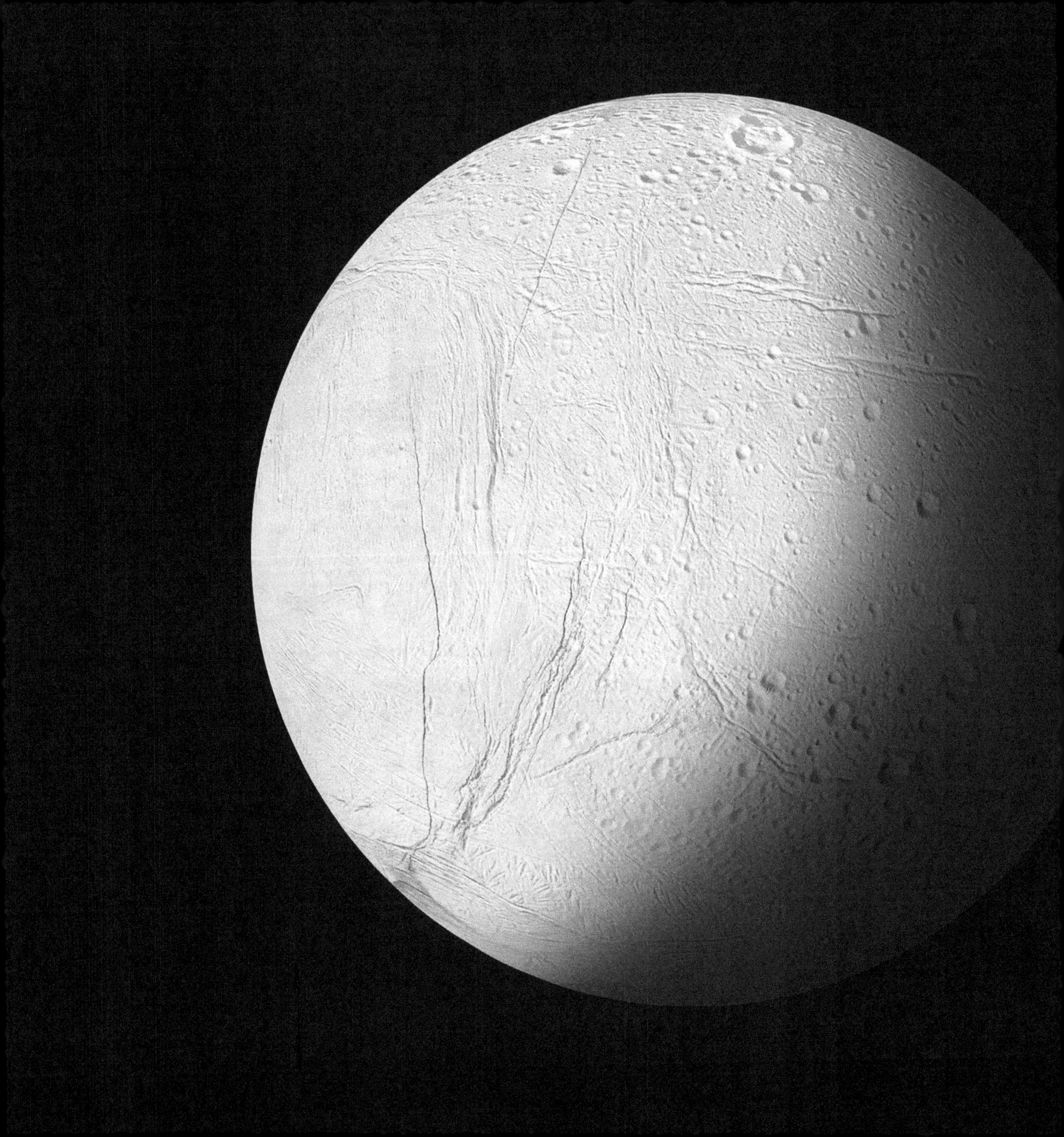

Triton is Neptune's largest moon. It is also the seventh largest moon in our solar system.

Proteus is Neptune's second biggest moon. It is one of the darkest objects in our solar system.

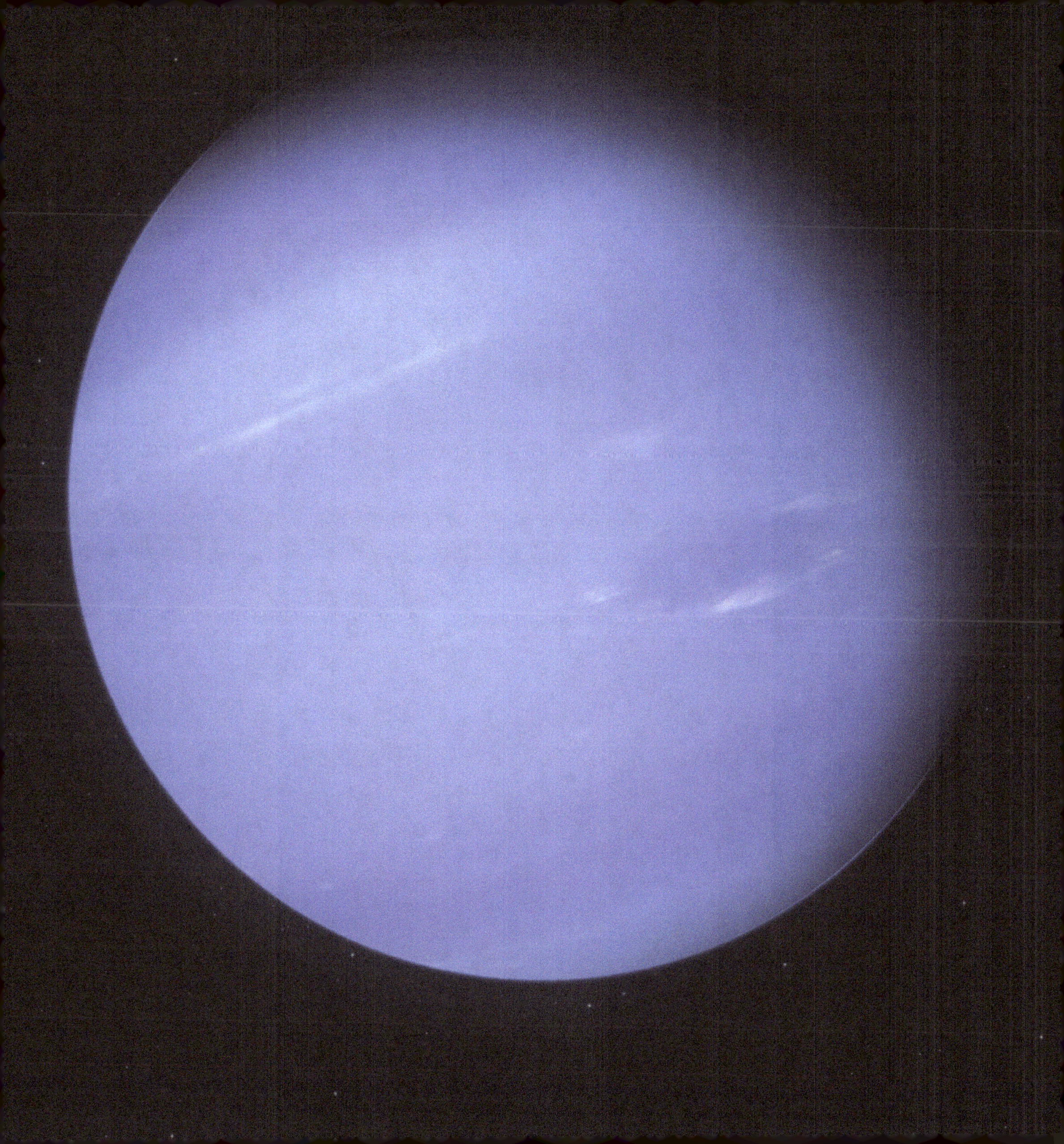

Charon is the largest moon of the dwarf planet Pluto. It was discovered by James Christy in 1978.

Did you enjoy reading?

Now it's time for you to share the things you learned from this book.

Visit

BABY PROFESSOR
EDUCATION KIDS

www.BabyProfessorBooks.com
to download Free Baby Professor eBooks and view
our catalog of new and exciting Children's Books

www.ingramcontent.com/pod-product-compliance
Lightning Source LLC
Chambersburg PA
CBHW082009160726

47999CB00008B/2766